# Chapter Introduction

I'm Marcus Mitchell, a twenty one year-old born and raised in Cornwall.

My upbringing wasn't difficult although it was sometimes challenging. I was still a very happy child growing up but had my difficulties which by then showed more as I progressed throughout my childhood.

I grew up on a small estate in my hometown of Camborne which I still live at to this day. We have a park right next to where we live, that was where I spent a lot of my childhood, playing with the other children next door. Although we were all best of friends most of the time, we would all fall out like cat and dog. I was mostly to blame though, admittedly because of the way I am and how I don't socialise as good as an ordinary child would. My socialising skills are very poor but that's just the way I am. I don't have as many friends as I feel I should have. I have always liked my own company and keeping myself occupied and entertained.

I would describe myself as a cheerful soul at the best of times but I certainly have a temper too. I get my down days most often, but who doesn't? I just have them more often than others. The trigger point for my down days are usually because I sometimes reflect on my lack of friends and social life. In an ideal world, I would like a happy, busy and sociable lifestyle. I always tell myself that I have my family and that's all that matters. My family always do their very best to help me as much as they can by taking me places, especially to my review meetings with CAHMS. I'm always thankful to my sister Charlotte for this, who is the eldest out me and my sisters, she's a massive support and always makes sure that I get there on time.

Most people who know me would also describe me as a polite and well-mannered young man. I've known when to say please and thank you (when I'm not having a meltdown or in a bad mood of course). Everyone always compliments my mum, Lisa on how well she has brought me up to be well-mannered and respectful, If it wasn't for my mum who knows what I would have turned out to be.

My family are my biggest supporters. They have always stood by me through thick and thin, even If I have said some very horrible and nasty things to them or physically hurt them during a meltdown. I'm very lucky that they still stand by me to this day, If it was any other way, I wouldn't have a loving family.

We aren't the biggest of families. We're quite a small and close bunch. I have three sisters. Charlotte, Lucy and Charlye. Charlye is the youngest. She's twenty two years-old and has got 2 daughters. Who's called Olivia, 5. And Evie,1. Charlotte is the oldest as she's twenty nine years-old and has two children named Kane, 9 and Lacey, 7. They are of course my niece & nephew too.

Last but, not least, I have another sister called Lucy, who is twenty five years-old. She also has two daughters called Ellie, 3 and Paige, who is not even 1.

My nephew and nieces are my world. I love them all the same equally. I couldn't be any prouder of them all. I'm very lucky to have them in my life and be the best Uncle they could ever have.

I'm also very close to all three of my sisters. We have a few ups and downs but I love them all the same. I have no real brothers or sisters. Charlotte, Lucy and Charlye are only my half-sisters but we think of each other as real brother and sisters.

Me, Charlotte and Lucy have different dads but we share the same mum whereas Charlye and me have the same dad but we don't share the same mum. It's all complicated, I know. I don't have any brothers although I wish sometimes I had. Having a family full of females can get a little annoying. To be able to have a brother the same age and sex would be a breath of fresh air. Having sisters, things can be too girly for my liking.

I also have another little sister named Alisha. She's the youngest of all being only six years-old but we don't see her because she lives too far away with her mum in Plymouth, around 60 miles away from us. It's a shame that we never see each other. It's a difficult situation and things are just too complicated between my dad and her mum.

Swiftly moving over to my five fury friends who I would like to mention in this book. Starting with my two dogs who are both Jack Russell's. We have Slumpy who is the eldest out of the two and then we have Jaygo who is the son. My dogs are my best friends, they know me and my mum better than anyone else and always know our feelings best and can always tell when something is wrong or if we are having an off moment. I can always picture the exact moment in my head when I was walking home from Primary School with my dad when my mum rung me to say that we have a brand-new addition to the family, "we have our very own puppy", she announced which made me the happiest child on earth, as you can imagine. This is one of my earliest memories from my childhood.

Not forgetting to mention my three cats too! Without them, my mum wouldn't be calling this house an animal farm. Having pets is what makes a house a home. The love you have for them is just indescribable. From the moment you wake up to the moment you go to bed, they are always there and the only ones you can rely on as well as family.

# Early Autistic Traits

My mum has always known how different I act compared to my sisters. When I think about it now I feel that my mum had an easy, uncomplicated life with my two sisters whereas I feel that I was more challenging and difficult to understand for her. I thank my mum for caring for me in the way I needed to be to suit my needs and never given up on me no matter how stressful this was for her.

One of the many difficulties that my mum experienced with me from day one was bath time. It would always be a struggle for her because every time I had a bath I would scream and cry until I gasped for breath as I didn't like bath time at all. I would constantly scream the place down from beginning to end. I didn't like being naked at all, I still don't like it now in fact as I feel uncomfortable from not having the support of wearing my clothes whereas I feel complete and comfortable wearing them. I think it's also because I'm very conscious of my weight too.

One of my difficulties that I can remember was wearing anything made without cotton. I absolutely hated the feel of anything else other than cotton. I couldn't physically wear a top with totally different material. I knew that cotton was soft and that's what made me feel comfortable.

It was always very costly for mum because I was very fussy with materials. If I didn't like the feel of that particular material then it would be straight off and I wouldn't wear it ever again. Mum had to also make sure that my t-shirts were clean and fresh to wear more than once as most of the time I would only wear a particular top because I knew it felt right to me which lead to washing the same top daily. This wasn't because I was spoilt; it was simply because of my autism.

When I think about everything that my mum has told me about when I was young, it all suddenly springs to mind. I can still remember certain aspects now.

Every evening when I was ready for bed, instead of lying over my clean sheets, I would prefer to lie on a blanket because I hated the feeling of touching a crumb or find a strand of hair stuck to my sheets. The feel would irritate me and make me think my bed was dirty. I tried to distract myself from the thought but it never worked. Even now if I sleep in a completely different environment, e.g. school trip or in a hospital, I would think the bed was unclean! Also to know that someone else has used the same bed or sheets makes me feel disgusting and dirty.

The list is endless, it could go on forever! My mum told me that I always used to go to bed wearing only one sock without fail! It sounds strange but it was a habit that I just couldn't break, It was almost like a ritual. Mum would laugh when I go downstairs for breakfast and she would notice I am only wearing one sock! I did this for ages.

Something that is still very fresh in my mind was the times when I could walk on my toes. It may sound painful but to me it really wasn't. I would stroll across the lounge showing off to my family what I could do; they always cringed and asked me If It hurt which it honestly didn't! My toes would be tucked under my feet and I would just stroll to the other side of the room with not even one expression to show that it hurt. I can never do this now when I try, it is very painful!

When I was still very young, I couldn't role play with toys, e.g. action figures or in my case, my Tweenies' figures. If you don't have a clue what the Tweenies are, they are human-like puppets from the Cbeebies show, The Tweenies. I wasn't like most children that would role play; I didn't have an imagination and wouldn't know how to

play with them. I was absolutely mad on Tweenies! I had every bit of merchandise of the show you could ever think of, like old-school videos, books, CD's games, you name it! I had everything.

My concentration wasn't the best either. I didn't really enjoy all the usual children's activities like, painting, drawing or general learning. I lost interest very quickly within 10-15 minutes within doing the activity. I am sometimes still the same now but very little of it. If I watch a film that was around 2 hours long, I get very agitated but that depends how focused I am into the film or how much I'm enjoying it. The longest I could sit and watch a film is around 1hour 30 minutes. I can't watch a film in the cinema if It's is too long as I would start to fidget or become irritated. I would rather watch a film at home, in my own environment so if I get bored, I can easily switch it off when I've lost interest.

At the age of three, my mum noticed that my speech wasn't clear so I underwent speech therapy in my local clinic. I can't remember a huge amount of this as I was too young to remember. The speech therapist asked me to pronounce sounds to try to improve my speech, also when I spoke I used to curl my tongue which sounded like I had a lisp. Although this helped, my speech mostly corrected itself with age.

I also had several hearing tests because I was used to having the volume high while watching television at home so they checked if I had any hearing difficulties which I did. Therefore I had to have grommets fitted into my ears as I had too much wax built up inside. I can remember one trip to the clinic though. I can slightly remember hearing puppets with rattles, rattling behind my back just to check if I had any difficulties hearing sounds around me. I didn't enjoy it at all, I was screeching because I hated it so much. My mum was surprised that I remembered this in fact!

I didn't like strange or sudden noises. I used to cover my ears with my hands. My mum had to warn me when she started hovering so I could either cover my ears or locate to another room in the house. The noise was too loud for me.

I had very little independence by the age of four. I didn't have an imagination when prompted to do something by myself e.g. personal care, getting myself dressed. Being motivated didn't help either, it didn't help at all. I don't think I was being lazy; it was that I couldn't concentrate enough to cooperate.

My mum had to repeat herself frequently when she asked me to do something and would have to shorten sentences to help me understand. This still applies today because I lose concentration and too much information causes my mind to overload which makes me anxious, irritable and respond less. It's almost like my brain shuts down because I can't take any more information.

I didn't really have a lot of interests when I was little; I wasn't sociable like I should have been. Now when I look back to those days, It was all about watching videos, playing with toys etc. But now I look at my Nephew & nieces today, it's all technology and game consoles which we didn't have as much back then.

I couldn't grasp simple tasks. One of these is learning to tie my shoe laces. I could only wear Velcro shoes up until secondary school and even today I still can't tie my shoe laces! It had taken me until I'd reach secondary school to tell the time whereas I should have learnt how to do this in Primary School. I know how to tell the time now. I first started to tell the time half-way through my time in secondary school.

I didn't have the best relationship with food. It was always a struggle when trying certain foods. I was a very fussy child. When mum introduced new foods to me, she would have to encourage me to try to eat a particular food by compromising with treats which didn't really work. I didn't even attempt to taste it, I wouldn't even try to chew it, I just rolled it on my tongue and spat it out. This was because I didn't like the texture of the particular food; I am still like this now; especially with vegetables! I'll admit that I am more of a junk food lover rather than healthy foods. It's just the way I am.

Moving onto a different subject. I was a happy child although very hyper at times. My mum says I was always on the go like running around the place or would spend a lot of time tripping over things. You could say that I was a very clumsy toddler! Tripping over would always result in cutting my knees. I was a little bit of a wimp when It came to hurting myself! If it was the tiniest scratch, I would always feel sorry for myself. There would always be a scratch, bruise or cut to show for it, looking back now I should have been wearing safety gear at all times, It was that bad...

Bedtime was sometimes a battle. I would never rest at night because I had a lot of energy inside me. It would take watching a DVD or having a book read to me would chill me out but It didn't always work.

One of my main habits was licking my lips. I couldn't stop! It was again another habit of mine. This would result into having breakouts of sores around my mouth where I licked my skin that much; it would dry out and turn painful. This would then turn into impetigo. I can't remember this at all! I don't have the greatest memory of my early ages although it sometimes seems familiar when my mum mentions it now.

Something that I can remember was when I had tantrums when somebody told me no. I didn't like the word no which I still don't now still as my family says! The tantrums would also show when I couldn't have anything done right away which again is something that still happens now occasionally. For instance if I wanted dinner cooked now, I would want it now or I would kick off. I never got my own way. Mum tried to be firm with me and would always tell me right from wrong but I wouldn't always agree. I was very dependent on my mum and would always be around her which she didn't get much time to herself.

My sisters were very girly and as the only boy in the family I think I wanted to join in so I would try on girl's shoes or wear dresses. I would even sometimes wear make-up which I just wanted to try out and put myself into my sister's shoes because I was mainly only surrounded by girls in my family. I was the only boy. My sister, Lucy would doll herself up to go out with her mates and I would just sit there on her bed watching her apply make-up or style her hair. I would be fascinated by it. She would then tell me to get out of her room because she liked having her own space without me, her little brother being in the way. This was always fascinating to me as I wondered what it was like to do girly things.

# Meltdowns

My behaviour is certainly something that has become a huge part in mine and my family's lives.

I didn't behave normally like I should of at the age of five; It was certainly a struggle for me to control my anger. This wasn't an everyday issue although there was a pattern in the way I behaved.

My behaviour difficulties started at the age of five around the time of starting Primary School but became more of a regular thing at home. The simplest things would make me agitated, then angry; the common cause of my meltdowns was being told 'no' or if I couldn't get my own way which will lead to myself suddenly exploding and having a huge tantrum that was uncontrollable. It took me at least an hour to calm down, or if not more. I have only now learnt that these tantrums are known as meltdowns.

When I was told no, I would respond badly. It is normal for a child to respond badly to the word 'no' but I would react to the extreme. By not getting my own way, this would lead to kicking, shouting and even biting. On most occasions, I would bite which must have been very embarrassing for my family when I look back now, especially when this happens in the supermarket! Whenever I kicked off, my parents had to escort me to the car. At this point I would be kicking and screaming and passers-by would be intrigued to know what was happening or just stare at me in disgust. I was even judged, they would be mumbling under their breath at how naughty I was but it's all down to struggling to communicate

It was hard to control my behaviour, I also used to say hurtful and nasty things to my family in the heat of the moment which then I instantly regret and always thought I shouldn't have said that. What I would say would be very hurtful and to the extreme e.g. wishing death on people or something really personal. I still occasionally say hurtful things now without thinking. It takes a lot for somebody to say something like this but for me it's easy to say and not feel any remorse. Afterwards when I've had time to reflect on my behaviour, I regret it instantly and think 'Did I honestly say something as hurtful as that?'

As I grew older, my temper became even worse to a serious extent. It became too uncontrollable; everything that came out of my mouth was disgusting and extremely hurtful to my family. It was like I was possessed or gone completely mad.

For my mum, it felt like living on egg shells and she would be in fear that I would have another huge meltdown. Mum would be up at stupid times of midnight clearing up broken glass or objects. She always felt like this because I smashed ornaments that belonged to our house and she couldn't afford to replace the things I damaged.

I would reach for any nearest object and then it would suddenly fly across the room in seconds. Something I am still disappointed in myself now was the times I threatened people with knives. It got that bad, mum had to hide every single knife away in the kitchen because she feared the worst would happen.

I would even hold a knife up to my family. Now when I think back, I can't imagine how terrifying this must have been for my family to be involved in such a dark situation like this!

I become so abusive I had to be restrained on the floor to protect others and myself. I must of turned into some kind of animal because I would growl and dribble. My face would turn bright red and my eyes would be in blood shock. That's how angry I must have been. Mum was told to use different techniques to help calm me down as It took hours for me to come around to my normal self again. I would just be in my own little world not knowing what was going on around me. Mum was sometimes worried because I would often blackout and faint during a meltdown when I'm feeling my most tensed. There would be no life in me for no more than 20 seconds and mum would be tapping me for a response until I came back around,

My life soon changed for the better of me and my safety when services persuaded mum to contact the police if matters ever got worse. She had no other choice but to, to keep me and everyone else safe.

I remember a particular incident when I was being restrained by my mum's partner and a police officer came to the house to try and talk to me but I was having none of it, shouting, kicking and screaming. The worst soon came when I finally stepped out of line and physically spat in the police officer's face. I finally blew my chance when it came to my surprise when they arrested me. I was convinced they couldn't arrest an eleven-year-old kid but I was totally wrong. When I heard them say I was under arrest, I couldn't help but feel heartbroken and actually thought I was going to be locked away forever! The policeman placed handcuffs around my wrists and then I was escorted to the police station.

When I arrived at the police station, I was thrown into a bare cell. This definitely didn't feel like my usual surroundings which by then

I finally realised and had time to reflect on the incident that night. I was bored to death just staring into space wondering if I'll ever come out.

Hours after, I was told I had to stay with a foster family overnight just until everything had blown over and it was safe to return home. I spent most of the night sobbing and eventually realised how serious this had become. When I had finally calmed down and had time to reflect, everything seemed like a blur and I told myself 'what just happened?!'. It was like I couldn't remember the incident and what had caused it.

Finally, I got some much needed help to try and control my temper with introducing some strategies. It was no help to me at the time because I knew that I needed professional help and not some kind of anger management to sort my issues out. I certainly needed better help in a way that suited my challenging behaviour.

This became a regular thing nearly every couple of months. From then forward, my behaviour spiralled out of control and my actions grew more aggressive and I was even tougher to handle. At this point mum even doubted that I may do something to the extreme so she had to protect herself and others for their safety of me.

I remember once it was morning and I'd just got out of bed. I opened my bedroom door as normal leading out onto the hallway of upstairs, I realised mum had set an attachment on my door so she could hear If I woke up. She did this because she feared for her safety as I was threatening to kill my family. This is something named intrusive thoughts which I'll explain more about further into the book. Even though mum believed that I wouldn't do such a thing, there was always that chance that she could have been wrong If she'd have ignored it.

Looking at what happened back then and what must of went through mum's head does actually upset me to think that she wasn't safe in her own home because she believed her own son would do something as bad as that. She had to keep herself safe even if it meant going the extra mile because I was quite mentally unstable.

By this point I started to self-harm because I thought this was the only way out from feeling like this. I become extremely depressed at this point.

I would dig into my skin with something sharp until I bled to the extreme. I always take my anger out on myself because I blame myself for most things. Self-harming is something I've always done after a meltdown, I feel like it releases the anger from me which is not ideally the best thing to do.

I try as much as I can to find better strategies for when I get angry but they never really work with me, e.g. count to ten or punch a pillow. It's easier said than done!

Harming myself is a difficult habit to break and it feels like the only option. it's hard to break that habit. It's kind of like a kid that can't live without sweets!

What I eat has a huge effect on my behaviour. I am more of a junk food kind of person than the healthy type. My family can notice the difference as soon as I eat chocolate; chocolate is my downfall because it changes my mood from feeling upbeat to depressed. I would say that I am an emotional eater; I always turn to junk food if I am having a down period or if I've had a bad day.

It was Christmas Eve by now, 2015. I had fallen out with my half-sister, to whom I was very close to. I didn't see her until New Year's Day and that was the day when my dad had tried to resolve matters by bringing us all together to talk, except it wasn't as easy as that and we all argued. Bringing us together to talk about things was way too soon because our fallout was still fresh. Originally, our fallout was because we had grown distant with each other and we would just often pick at each other and be down each other's throats. She had her twelve month old daughter to look after so that was the reason why we grew distant. Don't get me wrong, I love my niece. I and my sister had only grown closer because she was pregnant with my niece and she moved into a flat just seconds away from my front door. We would all spend so much time together and I would help her with my niece and be there for support whilst her partner would be at work. We did everything together. We had similar interests and we are similar in age by 2 years between us. In the end, I sometimes questioned whether I was too close to her because I had to remember my sister, her partner and my niece needed their time as a family.

While I continue to write this this chapter at this moment, I have had a stressful and emotionally draining week. It's been tough due to several reasons. Mum is struggling to take care of our second family pet, Jaygo who is a miniature Jack Russell. He is my heart and soul but is a handful! He has so much energy; he's like a live wire. Mum was planning to rehome him due to him messing everywhere in our house and for reasons of her own. Mum is struggling to bend etc. when she gets up in the morning, which is due to her recent diagnosis of having the condition fibromyalgia; therefore, it hurts her having to get down on her knees to scrub the floor clean where the dog has fouled. As much as she adores him too, she wants the best for him and that's to live on a small farm so he can burn his energy and at the same time will help de-stress her life to help her cope with the illness she's got.

Of course, I wasn't the happiest person alive, so me and mum was having endless amounts of discussions about the dog but I kind of came to terms that it would be better for Jaygo to go and have the best life possible on a family farm with other animals and children. The day after the decision was made, mum had found a suitable home for my dog. So, off he went that evening after I had said my tearful goodbyes to him. However, the morning after he had gone my mum had received a message from the new owners, they said Jaygo would have to be returned to us as he had continuously fouled around the house during the night. I was happy to hear this as it meant he was coming back home to us where he belongs.

It was a Sunday afternoon and Jaygo had returned home but mum was still adamant that the dog will be rehomed. I desperately tried to prove to her that I would take the dog for walks and take better care of him myself. Later on, during the day, my sister, niece and nephew had come to visit us. My sister sat beside me at the dining table whilst mum was preparing an evening meal. Charlotte spoke to me about the idea of the dog being rehomed and had said that the dog was not walked enough and it was unfair for him to stay as I hadn't made an effort before to walk him often. The conversation became very heated and I could feel myself becoming very anxious which then resulted in me becoming angry and verbally abusive towards charlotte. I had questioned her parenting skills and said some offensive things to her.

Within that time and whilst mum was cooking, mum had received a phone call. She answered the phone but went to the garden to talk to the person on the other end of the call. She then returned to the kitchen and had said it was my cousin. We had seen her within the last week or so and she had said she and her partner would consider having the dog to keep him in the family still. Mum had said that she would like to have the dog and that I could visit the dog whenever I wanted to. For a split second, I agreed then straight away after remembering a remark that I had taken the wrong way by my cousin on a Facebook status that I had wrote the day before. I said no she cannot have him. I then became more anxious as mum was still adamant that she wanted to rehome him.

My sister and mum then tried to explain that I had got it all wrong and within that my mum's partner had come into the kitchen and said "your mum has decided and it's your mother's choice, not yours!"

Well what can I say, that was like throwing a red rag to a ball coming from him as mine and Clifford's relationship is much to be desired. I then replied "you love this and can't wait for the dog to go" and he replied with a hand gesture meaning yes, can't wait! That was it by then; I had suddenly exploded and shouted very personal remarks like death threats. I was too angry to think before I spoke so I launched a full mug of tea across the room without thinking what the consequences would be especially with my dogs treading on the glass and hurting themselves.

Clifford then got aggressive and got closer into my face. I didn't like it so I grabbed his face with my hands, forgetting that I was digging my nails into his skin and then pushed him away from me. Then he suddenly punched me on the side of my face leaving me feeling like I have a golf ball stuck out of my face, It happened too quick to feel the pain. Mum looked shocked and shouted "get out of this house the both of you!"

I ran upstairs to my bedroom feeling like a ball of fire. Without thinking again, I smashed my against my head thinking it would knock some sense into me. I thought to myself 'I must have a tough head!' because it didn't knock me out. I couldn't control my emotions so I grabbed a piece of broken glass and started scratching it against my arm until I hoped the pain would go away. Blood was dripping everywhere at this moment so I ran downstairs in a rage, Clifford was still giving it large to me. I remember saying "look at my face!" in a temper. The side of my face was bruised and swollen. I didn't understand why he would do this. As I grabbed my coat from the cupboard, I banged my head several times on the door trying to knock some sense into me and tried to calm myself down but it didn't get me anywhere and I was just left with a bruised and swollen forehead.

I ran to next door to talk to my next-door neighbour called Sue. We went indoors and sat down and I spoke to her about what had just happened while tapping the open wounds on my arm with a wet cloth. By this point, I was calm. Mum had phoned the ambulance to check my injuries and made sure I was ok, which I was fine. The police came too, so I explained everything that had happened that early evening. They took me to my dad's house over the road to let things settle until it was safe to return home again.

A few hours after the incident that night, my mum and I had a little chat about how I'm feeling at the moment, which I wasn't in the best of moods. We had a bit of a heart-to-heart if you'd like to call it! That's what mums are there for. This was the first time in a while I have opened up to her and tell her how I was feeling but it was good to get it off my chest. It was just everything that had got on top of me with the dog being rehomed and overwhelmed by the college London trip coming up.


This wasn't the best half-term I had in mind. A day later, the same time of evening at around 6.00pm, Clifford returned home from work. I had no intention in forgiving him for punching me so I just pretended he was never there. We were all sat in the kitchen when mum looked at Clifford and said 'See what you've done to his face!' Mum didn't help the situation and should of left it when it all suddenly got out of hand yet again. Me and Clifford started arguing again by throwing remarks at each other. You're probably thinking how childish this is that an adult and child are arguing about who was right or wrong but this is what it's like. He told me to grow up and then I suddenly blown and lobbed another mug sitting next to me at the kitchen table across the room leaving the kitchen soaked in tea.

Mum exploded and told me off. I and mum were fighting as I ran into the lounge threatening to smash up the house. Clifford then restrained me and didn't realised he was actually hurting me. It took me a while to calm down so mum phoned the police. I became really aggressive by spitting and hitting out. It shouldn't have got this far.

When the police arrived, I was still furious as I continuously smashed my head purposely against the floor not thinking how much damage I could do. Mum is always telling me that one day I am going to seriously injure my head by banging it every time. When I look back I can't believe how easily this had all started. I always blow very quickly and it won't take much!

The police restrained me to stop me from bashing my head; I was held on the floor with a cushion under my head to keep me safe. I wasn't responding to anyone at all, maybe it was a shock? I continuously bit my hand digging my teeth into my skin until I was bleeding. I didn't speak to anyone, I just ignored everyone, the police, mum and her partner couldn't get a response from me as I ignored them all. This took a while for them to get through to me. I was sitting in the middle of the lounge with a cushion covering my face because I was too embarrassed to look at them all in the eye. I came around about three hours later at 9.00pm that evening. I was calm in the end when the police left. Afterwards I just chilled out on the sofa reflecting on my behaviour, I was very ashamed at how bad I had become.

The next few days I had constant meetings with social services as they came to my house to talk about the latest meltdowns. They noticed the side of my face had a bruise so I told them that mum's partner had punched me. They noted everything down onto paper. My mood over those few days suddenly took a huge turn, I was feeling incredibly low. I hated myself and didn't want to be around anymore because everything had got too much for me. I thought that I couldn't live like this, kicking off every five minutes, I felt very suicidal. I was feeling emotionally drained and tired after a few tough days.

Social services had to involve child protection because of the injury on the side of my face of what mum's partner had did to me. He was advised not to come over to the house for a while until everything had settled. I had endless amounts of talks with my social worker about pressing charges on Clifford for hurting me, but I don't think I can do something like that because I feel guilty and I don't want to make my mum unhappy and sad because I've ruined her relationship although she did tell me to do whatever I thought was best.

It's been another few days now and It was a normal college day and I was feeling pretty miserable. I had a little catch up with my social worker about whether I should press charges on my mum's partner for hitting me in the face. It hasn't been smooth and delightful at all since then.

On Monday evening, I returned home from College as normal at 5:00pm feeling miserable. I was deep in thought about whether I should take actions further from the incident as it was playing on my mind a lot. My evening was very chilled until my dad popped over to see me as he has just been away on holiday to Cardiff to see relatives. He asked me why I didn't reply to his message the night before but I was busy.

By this point I was already in a mood. I was a little snappy as it was a busy day at college. I was feeling very down so I went to grab some pills from the cupboard to attempt taking a load of pills because everything got on top of me. My dad managed to stop me and of course, I wasn't impressed. I suddenly saw red and grabbed the kettle next to me and thrown it in a rage before running upstairs into my bedroom to calm down. From this moment in time, I was raging like a bull and smashed my bedroom to pieces breaking my personal belongings including my mirror (Yes, I know seven years bad luck unfortunately)

My mum thought this got way out of control so she thought she would do the appropriate thing and call the police to keep me safe again even though it hasn't been long since the last meltdown. I feel like the past few weeks have been exhausting and very horrible. By the time the police arrived into my bedroom, dad had restrained me. I wouldn't calm down so they handcuffed me. I was a wreck after I finally calmed down. I was suddenly arrested for criminal damage and domestic abuse. Luckily my mum and dad never pressed charges on me. They took me straight to the police station and thrown me into a cell for the night. I remember thinking things just can't go on like this. I need to stop and think of things I can do to prevent this from happening again. Being locked up in a cell at the police station is horrible. I felt like my whole world had come crashing down.

When I was released the next day in the afternoon I was taken to a foster placement as I couldn't return home as everything was fresh still. The foster family was so friendly and treated me so well. They were really lovely although it wasn't the same as being at home with my family, where I should belong.

Two days passed and I am now at home with my family where I belong. This was certainly one of the worst experiences of my life. It's now time to turn a new leaf. I feel absolutely awful and regret everything I've put my family through. I feel like a huge let down and an embarrassment.

It's Halloween, 2016, and nothing is going my way. I've spent all night upstairs in my bedroom trying to get some video footage for my blog. I was doing a bedroom tour but it just wasn't going as well as I had planned it. After spending many hours of recording my video, it was my first time of 'vlogging', so they call it. (video blogging), then unfortunately all the footage I thought I had saved had accidentally been deleted. I've wasted all my time to do something for absolutely nothing, I thought. I'd put a lot of time into doing this for it all to be wasted.

I was furious so I went down stairs into the kitchen. "Want anything for tea?" my mum said to me. I snapped at her as everything was just an overload of frustration. I told my mum furiously, "I've lost all of my video footage!".

Mum was busy and told me to calm down because I was becoming too overwhelmed with anxiety. I just wouldn't take it for an answer and I could feel myself getting more and more anxious until the moment I finally exploded and launched my drink across the kitchen.

Mum was annoyed and shouted "what was all that for!". I was told to clean up the mess but I wouldn't, I refused. Mum was repeatedly telling me to clean it up but now I had decided to throw all of my food across the floor too.

That was it. By now I was angry that I could barely talk without shouting and I could feel myself sweating and feeling hot. I grabbed a kitchen knife from the drawer, digging it into my skin as much as I could until I was bleeding.

"Why are you doing that for?" mum said and told me to stop it before I do some serious damage to myself. At the time, I wasn't listening and didn't care. Shouting at the top of my voice, I screamed, "I'm going to kill you, just drop dead!"

Smashing absolutely anything in sight including, the kettle, picture frames on the wall. I was livid but I hardly had any reason to be. Stabbing holes into the kitchen surface, my mum's partner rang the police and demanded a police officer to come out as soon as possible. Without hesitation, I ran to the front door and chased my mum's partner up the path with the kitchen knife still in my hand intending to stab him.

Mum was outside pleading with me to calm down. I just wouldn't stop, I was raging.
Flashing lights were in sight and I could hear sirens pulling into the estate with the neighbours watching aside from their windows. It soon hit me and I was convinced I was going to be locked up for a very long time.

Running back into the house, I thought the damage is done and there's no going back. I slammed the kitchen knife onto the unit before running back outside. The cop shouted "put the weapon down!". "I don't have anything on me!" I shouted back.

The police officer came over and handcuffed me. What I had done completely sunk in at this point and I was deeply sorry for my actions but it was way too late for that whilst sobbing my heart out.

I was shoved into the back of the police van and all I could think is what happens now? It was gone past 11pm and I was taken into police custody and was placed in a cell for the night. What a coincident, I thought. I never intentionally planned this for Halloween. It just unexpectedly happened on this particular day.

# People Obsessions

Throughout my life I have always had interests just like anyone else, but there is a difference between interests and something of interest that can control your everyday life.

Is that good or bad I ask myself? this is a part of my Autism and OCD that I'm trying to understand myself even now and as I write this book.

My very first obsession was with a guy who was friends with my sister.

It all began through Facebook. I was randomly drawn to this guy in some way, I needed someone to talk to because of the way I have been feeling lately, someone that doesn't know me who wouldn't judge me and would understand me. I don't entirely know what attracted me to him in the first place, maybe I kind of had a thing about him because he was attractive?

I was constantly checking his profile on Facebook and messaging him asking If we could have a chat. I would constantly message throughout the day as If I had nothing to do all day long other than chat to people but I didn't quite understand that they could be busy getting on with their life. Now when I look back, I feel like I was some weirdo or a stalker, I feel ashamed of myself.

He was puzzled as to why some random is messaging him. It was so out of the blue. He also didn't want any contact with me because he thought I was strange. I was up at stupid times of the night as I couldn't sleep. I think I was confused with my sexuality too; my mind was all over the place. I couldn't sleep at night; this person was on my mind 24/7 to the point of going insane. It got extremely obsessive, I didn't realise how obsessive it all was until now, it's mad. I managed to find out his address so I sent him endless amounts of anonymous letters just so I could explain why I'm so interested in him although it was all utter ridiculous. I used any excuse to get to know him and have a reason to get in touch.

It got extremely out of hand at this point when I created a fake profile on Facebook pretending to be a female hoping to attract his attention. I would flirt as this 'pretend' beautiful female but really it was me, an insecure teenager looking to find their way in life making friends and socialising. I would spend hours on my phone; mum was concerned and knew something was wrong as I was constantly on my phone all day, every day. This was so out of the norm and very unhealthy.

This took over my life and my whole life spiralled out of control, It got that bad. My emotions were everywhere when they had no reason to be. I had endless amount of dreams at night dreaming of us being together, you may be thinking this is strange but I couldn't help my thoughts, it was uncontrollable, It was really messing with my mind. I felt that If I couldn't be friends with him then I was convinced I had no choice but to commit suicide to get his attention. I became very depressed. I just wanted to be involved in his life. I can't imagine how he must of felt. It must have been annoying for him and must of felt a little confused and unsure of his safety.

One evening when I arrived home after a busy day at school, I grabbed a knife from the kitchen and wandered out looking around the area hoping to bump into him with a kitchen knife hanging out of my jacket's pocket. It became like a deadly obsession, quite literally. I was unsafe and my mental health was unstable. I thought that If I can't get through to him then no one can so I was planning on doing something drastic with this knife. I had a little secret crush that turned deadly dangerous. My mum didn't know anything about this because I told my mum that I was only going to the corner shop.

I somehow managed to retrieve his number from his Facebook profile after snooping through his profile for some time. I was constantly calling him and would then hung up because I was too nervous or even too scared to tell how I felt because I was embarrassed. I just wanted to tell him how I feel about him but he didn't want to know whatsoever which frustrated me a little.

My family was notified by him after that. He told my sister about the situation and how concerned and worried he was. That evening I set off with my backpack and belongings hoping to escape and run away from the situation as I was too embarrassed to confront my mum at home. I remember walking down a back lane hoping to find a little alley to sleep in for the night, I was convinced that I could somehow move to London, my happy place, to escape everything as it became too much to bare. I was really mentally unstable. I soon returned home as I changed my mind because I had nowhere to hide and nowhere to go. The only place to be was at home.

When I arrived home, mum was worried about me and wanted to know everything. She wasn't angry, she was just concerned for me like any mum would be. She was worried about my state of mind. I told her everything that was going on and by this point she knew that it was time to get me the help that I desperately needed.

I attended several therapy sessions to help me control my thoughts. The services that helped just couldn't give us the answers as to what could potentially be wrong with me. I finally got the help I needed when I was sectioned under the mental health act later that year where I was diagnosed with OCD, I'll explain more on that during the book later.

My obsessions became more frequent a few months later, it was becoming a pattern. This time It was an obsession of interest. I have always enjoyed watching the soap opera, EastEnders. I became fixated on the programme but in a good way. It would always somehow slip into my topic of conversations with most people I talk to. I wrote many fan mails to my favourite cast members asking politely for their autograph. My favourite all-time character was Stacey and she still is my favourite character now. I was probably the biggest fan on this planet, I was an EastEnders geek as I like to call it. Watching it every night was a tradition of mine, I never missed an episode from the age of eight. I would always be ready sat on the sofa ready to get my daily fix of EastEnders. EastEnders certainly played a huge part of my childhood. Ask me absolutely anything about the soap and I would tell you there and then without even having the time to think about it. I was a true fan.

I don't watch it as much as I used to now although I still really enjoy watching it, I've lost interest. I'm also a huge fan of Hollyoaks and always dreamed of becoming an actor on the soaps.

As I grew older, my obsessions become stronger. I still don't really understand OCD as much as I should, It's just something I have never been able to understand because I choose not to. It has never sunk in that I have OCD until around now. It took a long while for me to get the head around it all but I'm getting much better now and I'm far more knowledgeable from my own experiences.

Opening up to someone is certainly something I don't feel comfortable with because I fear that I would be judged and hated which makes me feel embarrassed. I have never really been the type of person to show my true feelings. Not even to my family. I never show much compassion and affection. It's hard for me to tell somebody that I love them or give any form of love. I don't like hugging people because I get embarrassed. I've never been the one to show my feelings. I like to keep my thoughts to myself which can sometimes make me explode when I have too much going on in my head at once.

Having an obsession over somebody really messes with my head. No matter how hard I try to push it to the back of my mind, it comes back stronger and gets the better of me. It interferes with my everyday life to the extent of harming myself to try and stop the emotional pain that I feel. I cause harm to myself because I feel it's all my fault and It would be better for everybody If I wasn't around anymore. I can sometimes get thoughts where I question my presence and how much better I would feel If I was to suddenly die.

My obsessions are something that I certainly don't feel comfortable with talking about. This is a hard thing for me to do and I'm proud to be able to share this with you all. I'm so much better at writing my feelings down on paper than I am talking about them.

I was a huge fan of the reality TV show, The Only Way Is Essex. I'm still a fan now but not as much as I was then. Reality TV is something I really enjoy watching as it's real life and it's not scripted or although some people do think that it can be made up. My favourite star of the show was Mark Wright until he quit. I don't know what drawn me to like him although he always looked rather attractive. Maybe I admired his looks or even this could be my very first celebrity crush?

By then this turned out to become another obsession or fascination, as I like to call it. They became more frequent and got a lot more stronger to the point where It would interfere with my life.

I was totally fixated on him. Somehow, I dreamed of becoming closer to him in his inner circle of relationships. It's strange and something I can't describe very well. It's like a sudden fantasy that I can't control or even explain.

I imagined myself playing a huge part in his life, someone that would mean a lot to him. My mental state was out of control and I feel way out of normality just writing about it. I've never really discussed this with my family as I'm not very good with talking about my feelings to people as I mentioned before. I don't even like sharing my feelings to counsellors or people in that kind of field.

One Friday evening once I've finished school, I took my dogs for a stroll through the fields. I was trying to come up with an idea of trying to get in touch with Mark Wright who was this massive current celebrity and had a huge fan base that it was so difficult to get in touch with him directly without having to go through an agent or manager. I searched the internet far and wide for a contact number, trying to find a local company of where he hangs out, like a nightclub or restaurant. So I found the contact details for a local nightclub which features on The Only Way Is Essex, it's s a TOWIE hotspot in Essex. I saved the number in my phone that afternoon at school. I was determined to get some sort of contact with him even if it sounds deluded, I don't care. As I stroll through the fields that evening with my dogs I couldn't wait any longer to make this phone call so I rung the place hoping they would help me. As I got through to them, I made up some story of pretending to be a long- lost brother of his. I know, It sounds mad but my mental state obviously wasn't good. I got a little nervous and started to flutter my words as I speak so I hung up, feeling embarrassed. I never rang again since then as I didn't pluck up the courage to put myself through it again.

My obsession went on for months on end. I found a photo of Mark Wright in a celebrity magazine that I'd buy weekly so I cut out the photo and carried it around with me in my pocket so I could just stare into his eyes whenever I looked at it and so it could be a constant reminder. I was deeply fixated and felt like one of those celebrity stalkers or super fans.

As weeks went by, this whole obsession disappeared luckily. I pushed it to the back of my mind and replaced it with other happier things to think about. It finally worked. It naturally wore off after this and I never thought no more of it. I don't know how I managed to do it but It was definitely a relief for me and I managed to get back to my happier self for a while. Even now If I say the name 'Mark Wright' I get goose bumps and feel uncomfortable because it's a reminder of my obsession that I had. It's not that I hate him, it's just thinking about it all which I don't want to ever go back on that rollercoaster ride again. I am still a very good fan of his now but not as much as I did back then.

I get by with my life for a while thinking I've finally beat my obsessions and I have. It feels so good to finally feel a little bit of normality again. I still haven't told my family about it all, I've kept it to myself for too long and only now I've finally feel comfortable in talking about it in this book.

Of Course by now I could never totally be free from my obsessions and of course, along came another one!

Later on and while attending secondary school there was a boy who was a few years above me in years. I was in year seven, aged eleven years-old. My sister was mutually friends with him. I got to know him when one time I was hanging around with my sister and her mates. He seems like a really great guy and very friendly to me whenever we passed through the corridor and would always say hello. I think I fancied him. I had a little crush. This was when I first became confused with my sexuality. I only really had one friend at school and once I had confided in him and our friendship changed. He grew uneasy around me and embarrassed but I got to be pushy towards him and repeatedly questioned our friendship.

My friend and I grew to despise each other and we became enemies. We would torment each other and call one another names whenever we passed each other in the corridor. My secret wasn't private for very long as rumours started spreading around the school about my crush on this boy that I fancied and I knew exactly who started it without even thinking about who it could be. I was furious and outraged that such a 'friend' of mine could do this to me.

We finally had it out with each other when we confronted one another in the same lesson which was Science. I told him I was not happy and felt betrayed. He denied ever starting the rumour but I could tell by his face that he started it. He was smirking and giggling at me. I was now like a ball of fire and we started fighting in the middle of our lesson. I pushed him off his stall and stormed out of the lesson. I was upset and angry. Everyone was laughing at me and I felt so humiliated and of course ashamed by my violent behaviour.

By the rumours reached him and he finally knows all about my little crush on him. I was embarrassed. I would try and sneak out of lessons early to avoid him in the corridor and spend my lunch and break with other friends in a classroom where the rest of the year 7's hung out. The time was finally here when I bumped into my him in the school corridor. I didn't make any fuss of it, I just totally blanked him because I was too shy and embarrassed to confront him. I think he tried to not think too much of it and dealt with maturely which I was pleased and thankful for.

I was deeply into him by now. I thought as he's fine about my crush on him, he would be fine with anything. It turned into being a little obsession once again. He would be constantly on my mind 24/7. I was convinced that my little fascinations was over by now and put behind me but I was wrong.

It was a Thursday late afternoon and was coming to the end of the school day. I was told to spend my lessons in the base which was a little hut where students work in if they're finding times tough or had troubles with being in class. By now history was repeating itself and I become obsessed with this boy I fancied. My work on the computer was complete so I had free time to myself. My school emails need checking so I checked them. All of a sudden I had a huge idea to send him an email explaining my desired love to him. Sort of like a little love letter if you would like to call it that. My mind was telling me to send it but my heart was telling me not to. So I went ahead and sent the email. I deeply regretted sending the email now and thought to myself that I have to face up to this sooner or later.

The bell rang and it was time to leave. I left the base and headed to reception to wait for a friend. It wasn't long until I passed him again. He was with his female friend. He sort of gave me an odd look which left me wondering if he'd read the email I sent him. I finally confronted him as he walked over with his pal. Oh no, I though. I've dropped myself in it now, this confrontation had to come sooner or later.

His friend came marching over asking me what that email was all about. Oh god I thought, It was meant to be read in private! Now I am deeply embarrassed. I responded by pretending that I didn't have a clue about this email which really, I did. I couldn't deny it anymore so I said I did send it. I was feeling very ashamed regretted my actions. Before she said anything I stormed off as I couldn't handle this any longer. As I walked off, I heard someone call me a weirdo which really upset me.

I thought now I couldn't ever return to school and face up to my problems. I refused to go to school for a few days and reflected on the mess I've got myself into. Then something suddenly came over me and I felt a surge of braveness. I've got myself into this mess so now I've got to get out of it, I said to myself.

By now me and my friend finally put our troubles behind us and carried on being friends by patching things up. But it wasn't how it was before, something has changed. My friend didn't really want to give me the time of day and lost interest in me but we were still civil and we spoke to each other every now and then.

I started feeling really down by now as I looked at reality and thought that nothing could ever go that far between me and my crush. My mind was telling me to end my life. I felt suicidal and lonely just because I craved attention from him. It sounds pathetic and stupid I know but this is how serious my OCD became. My mental state was a wreck.

I went to desperate measures and sneaked a pot of paracetamol into my bag. I was deeply craving his attention and was waiting for him to show interest in me. I emailed him the second time explaining that I was going to take an overdose and end it all once and for all to see if he's interested in me enough. I look back now and think it's silly that I took something like that too far but I suppose I didn't think like that back then. He must of alerted someone as I was told to go and see the pastoral support manager who is basically a support team who deal with situations like this.

I was told that he was concerned for my wellbeing and knew he had to alert a member of staff just to be on the safe side. I never intended to take an overdose, I suppose it was all for his attention which obviously worked.

My mum was now alerted and I was told to take some time out from school to get myself back on track. The school was deeply concerned about me and thought that it'll be the right decision to do a risk assessment on me. By now I realised this had gone too far.

My mum wanted me to start talking to her and give her some answers as to why I am acting like this. Of course I wasn't diagnosed with OCD at this moment so my mum didn't know what was wrong.

I now realised that this has all got too far and serious. It affected my future life at school because I was monitored more and got help with my issues. I attended anger mangment. which was a little help to move me in the right direction

A few weeks on and my obsession gradually faded as it usually does naturally. I was finally on the right track to improvement. I was finally cleared of my obsession which was a massive relief.

I'm not too sure on how I overcome my obsession. I wonder if they're ever fade when I'm going through one because it feels like it's impossible to shift.

I now haven't had an obsession for a good while. It feels great to not have one as it always pushed me to my lowest point and It's emotionally draining.

Along came another obsession. It's a pattern now, one would reoccur every so often. I know when I get one now and I can recognise the feelings I get. It still affects me big time but this new obsession wasn't drastic enough this time. Maybe it's because I'm getting older and finally getting more mature, I don't know…


I am a huge fan of the soap opera, Hollyoaks as I had mentioned previously. I watch it every night and have never missed an episode. I always enjoy watching it as it's the first television programme I have ever shown a massive interest in apart from EastEnders. I enjoy watching all soaps but Hollyoaks definitely does it for me every time. It's strange how so much drama in one small village there can be. I suppose it's because it's a soap and that's why I love it.

The character I most enjoy watching is Freddie Roscoe, he's sort of like a bad man whose very eye catching and definitely a piece of eye candy. By this point, I thought I had made up my mind of my sexuality. I'm more interested in males than females. So I'm bisexual or am I ? but I felt that I had made it clear to myself, either way id know my family would never turn their back on me for something like this as I know them too well not too. It's always been spoken about between me and my mum and the possibility that I may be bisexual

My liking for Freddie from Hollyoaks (aka Charlie Clapham) grew worse and I feel it becoming deeper and deeper. The more I watch Hollyoaks, the more I can feel a connection. He's become a huge part of my mind and even my life, it's frustrating all of a sudden.

This time round it isn't as strong as it has been in the past although I've still acted upon similar events.

One evening after college I was deep in thought. I've started to understand my OCD now so I thought I could share a little bit about it with him. It's kind of a positive obsession if you see what I mean. I'm more aware of my condition and I'm more confident sharing it with others. I saw this as a way of getting closer to him and using this as a good excuse by sharing my life story with him but more as a friendship way. I started penning a letter to him asking If I could share a little bit about myself with him and what it's like to live with Autism & OCD. I plucked up the courage to send the letter so I did. Two weeks later, I receive a letter back. I had butterflies inside my tummy hoping I could have a chance here. I opened it only to find a set of signed cards but no written letter of reply. I was extremely disappointed and saddened by this.

I thought to myself I must move on and forget about all of this. I managed to keep telling myself to let it go, maybe this was a start with managing my obsessions, who knows! I did finally let it go in the end. Luckily, this time round it was a short obsession but not as intense. I feel that now they are starting to disappear, I can get on with life instead of fantasising about something that is never going to happen in the first place.

# Life inside a psychiatric Unit

My life suddenly took a turn for the worse as my mental state spiralled out of control. Something wasn't right. My family were concerned by my sudden and extremely aggressive behaviour. They've never seen me life this before. I was a wreck. My meltdowns become a regular pattern in such a short space of time. My mood was all over the place. It didn't take much for me to get angry, It was literally over the slightest, silliest thing like my mum asking me to do something that I didn't want to do.

This wasn't long after my obsession with that guy my sister knew. My mental state was all over the place. Home life started becoming tough for me as there was a time I didn't get on with my mum. We would have rows in the house because I was told no if I was told to do something or I would respond negatively after I was told do so something I didn't like. I despised the word no. I'm still like that now to be fair but not as bad because I've matured with age over the years. But at this moment, there was suddenly a time where enough was enough as something had to be done, this was when I went through a rough patch and I was suddenly sectioned under the mental health act.

One evening in 2011, I had just had a meltdown. I can't remember much about what happened as it's still all a blur now. One thing I remember was when I was told I had to be admitted to The Priory, East Sussex, 300 miles away from my home in Cornwall. The Priory is a psychiatric unit for people who are suffering with mental illnesses although there were a lot of patients who also had a diagnosis of Autism. There was a mixture of both, some had mental health issues whereas others had learning disabilities.

Before I was admitted and before I was even diagnosed with OCD, I had been continuously washing my hands which was a huge problem for me and my family. That was one of the reasons why I was admitted. I didn't realise I had OCD back then before I was diagnosed at The Priory. Something in my brain was telling me to wash my hands which I believed they were always dirty and unclean. It wasn't until I got into a habit of washing them 24/7 that I felt they had started to feel extremely dirty. At the time I didn't think it was an issue, I thought it was normal for me to wash them every now and then which was around 40-50 times a day. My family could clearly see something was up and didn't want it to go unnoticeable before it grew worse. They would always say "that was the second time you've washed your hands in the space of 5 minutes you know", giving me a firm reminder.

It just became a usual thing. My hands became red raw after time and time. They were dry and cracked. It didn't hurt much although my skin became irritated from where they've become sore. I had obviously wiped away all my natural oils until my hands were bone-dry. On one occasion, I had even used bleach thinking I would have completely squeaky clean hands. They would burn like hell but at least I knew they were clean, I thought. I did anything to make my hands clean, even if it hurt me. My hygiene altogether became an obsessive thing which it then lead to me having 3 showers per day. It felt as If the world was going to end if I didn't wash them soon enough or something bad would happen if I didn't give them a quick clean. The signals to alert me to wash my hands or have a shower became very annoying. I started to feel that If my whole body felt dirty, I must wash my hands in order to feel better again.

I am a clean person anyway but maybe way too clean on a higher level. I think of myself as a clean freak because I would freak out if I didn't wash them immediately. It started to have a huge effect on me emotionally if I didn't have a shower or washed my hands. I became anxious or upset as washing my hands was the only thing that made me feel normal and better.

I will always remember that night I was parted away from my family when I had to get on my way to The Priory. It was the longest journey that I had ever been on before. I was extremely anxious and unsettled. The moment they told me I was going away to somewhere six hours away really hurt. To think I was that long away from my family literally killed me as I'm so used to being around them all the time. My family were obviously upset but thought It was the best thing to do, to get all the help I needed which I didn't receive at home, here in Cornwall. Further up the line, there is way better treatment because Cornwall is so limited to mental health resources and accommodation.

It was time to set off as the transport arrived outside my front door. This was very daunting and nerve wracking as this would be the first time I had spent the longest time away from home. As I got into the car I couldn't help but sob as I say goodbye to my mum. Not only my family, but my dogs too. My dogs are a big part of our family. It's strange to think how much love you have for your dogs. I absolutely adore dogs; they're definitely my favourite animal by far.

Sobbing in the backseat of the car I couldn't help but think if this could be the last time I see my family for a while. My mum always told me that the house was too quiet and empty without me in it as I was always around the house acting like a prat so there was a huge hole missing in the family. To be quite honest, the house wasn't the same without me. We are a very close family; we're always there for one another just like they are all there for me right now in my darkest of times.

The journey took at least 6 and a ½ hours. We took off very late in the evening at around 12.00am. My music kept me entertained throughout the whole journey. I love music. When I'm listening to music I feel like I'm in my own little world. It takes all my troubles away. Well, for at least 5 minutes or so!

The journey was ok I suppose although I was still feeling vulnerable and scared about what this experience might bring. I never thought positively at the time, I always thought negative as I never saw the good side of how this would help me turn a new leaf. It was a scary feeling like my whole life is about to suddenly change.

As the journey went by, we passed London. My favourite place. The place which makes me happy to think about. London has always been my favourite city. I've been there a few times with my family, it makes me think of the good times. I don't know why but I started to feel safe where I was as time went on because I was near London, which I guess was slightly overwhelming as well because I'm in a popular part of the country where a lot of things are happening and it's so busy. Cornwall is a lovely place to live, don't get me wrong but London has always been the place where I've dreamt of living. The atmosphere there is amazing and there's lots of things to do. I sometimes wonder what It might be like to live there as a celebrity. It would be incredible! To know that I am only a couple of hours away from Essex is cool as I was a massive fan of *The Only Way Is Essex*. It's strange to think I'm nearer to celebrities than I am back at home living in Cornwall. I see that as a good side of all of this, my mini holiday as I like to call it. I soon became more positive as time flew by.

I finally arrived at my destination at around 8.00am in the morning. which was the place that I was dreading of going to. I tried to think of it as a mini-holiday to forget the awful thoughts I was getting which was 'What If it's horrible like a prison?' or 'what if they treat you badly?'. As we drove up the path, my first thought was 'wow!'. This is huge! A big, white building which to me looked very old but grand. I was intrigued to see what it looked like inside as I thought it could be beautiful. But I was wrong, it didn't look awful, it was just something I didn't expect which I thought it'll be homelier. As we entered the reception area, it felt daunting. I was in this massive place which I wasn't familiar with at all. I wanted to go home but I had no choice but to stay here, who knew how long I could be here? Days, weeks or even months? At least however long, it's just until I get better and fully recover and feel back to my bubbly self again. I was tired and emotionally drained, All I wanted to do was go to sleep but in my own bed at home where I felt safe, secure and familiar.

Me and the guys who brought me here were greeted by a lady who seemed really lovely which took some of the negative thoughts away that I was thinking which made me think more positively in the end. She showed me up a flight of stairs to the first unit. It was kind of strange as every door was locked, bolted and secured. The doors had pass codes, there was not even one door without a lock. At least I knew I was safe and secure which is the main thing. That was all that mattered. We walked across the corridor as I was shown to my temporary bedroom. The bedroom was bare. It had a board of plastic over the windows so nobody could smash the glass to escape. There was a king size bed with some wooden units in the corners of my room to store my belongings. I didn't pack much with me as we all thought I would only be there for a week or so. I walked into the bedroom and made myself comfortable in this squishy, foam-material chair. Obviously, there was no plastic chairs as it needed to be a safe environment. I didn't think there would be a sink in there too, especially as I wash my hands too often. I washed my hands more because It almost like it was there for temptation.

A few hours passed by and I unpacked my belongings. I wanted to make it feel homely like it was my very own bedroom but I couldn't adjust to it as it was too soon. One of the nurses helped me unpack. As she emptied my bags she made a small pile of the things I wasn't allowed in my bedroom due to safety like sprays and sharp objects, the things that could put my safety at risk. I was cool with it although I was obviously gutted because I felt disappointed at the fact I was mentally unstable and was capable of anything. It felt uncomfortable that I wasn't trusted with many of my own belongings but I guess they couldn't risk it if I had done anything to harm myself or others. They just couldn't take that chance. This was my time to prove that I'm well and safe, There would be too much to lose If I had did something silly.

After we had unpacked everything, the nurse did a risk assessment with me. She asked me personal questions like 'Are you feeling at risk to yourself?'. I responded yes because my life couldn't get any worse than what it already was. I had dug a hole which was impossible to get out of so I had to lie in it and face up to my consequences. I knew that deep down they weren't there to laugh at me, that wasn't their job to, but it seemed that way. It seemed to me like they were there to judge me but that wasn't at all the case. They were professionals who are there to keep me safe and help me through my difficult patch but I couldn't see it at the time.

We spent around an hour just talking about why I was admitted. I spoke about my fascinations with people who I hardly knew which was one of several reasons to why I was admitted. It was hard to talk about but It seemed to get it off my chest. She was a great listener and made me feel comfortable. I mentioned that things had also got tough at home. I had more meltdowns and fell out with my family more than usual which was a major concern. Just by talking about everything helped me put it into perspective as to why I got to this point. It was a blur to me at that moment because so much had happened in the last couple of weeks, it sent my mind into overdrive. I was emotionally exhausted.

The first few days passed by. I seemed to feel a bit better now that I'd had got the rest I needed. The first night was tough as I didn't feel comfortable sleeping in a bed I wasn't familiar with and I was also a little home-sick. Most of my days were chilled as I spent a lot of days in the lounge where there was a TV and a few soft chairs scattered around. I don't think I could have lived without a TV! It sounds sad I know, but it's one of those things that make the place feel a little homelier although of course I knew that this wasn't actually my home. The usual was on the telly, soaps and entertainment shows, it kept us amused for most of my time there.

I got talking to many of the other patients who were here. They were ever so friendly to me. We would have discussions about our admissions which I was fine with sharing. It felt nice to know there were others here to talk to. We all had a lot in common too which was great. We were mostly around the same age although some were maybe a year or two older.

Throughout the days, the staff arranged activities for us to keep us entertained. We played a lot of sport even though it's not my kind of thing, but I still enjoyed it. Anything entertained me throughout my recovery as there wasn't a wider variety of things to do and you couldn't really pick or choose. Although the staff did their very best to keep us amused and entertained every day.

A few weeks into my recovery now and I finally feel more relaxed and comfortable. Being on my own in another part of the country is hard but I soon got over it as time went by. I got involved more with the other patients, we would have endless amounts of chats just talking about celebrity gossip. That was a good subject of interest we shared. I am a massive fan of celebrities so we spent hours on end talking about our favourite stars. Me and the others would be allowed to walk to the shop daily, as long as there was a member of staff with us to supervise. It was only down the road from us. Walks to the shops were really exciting for us as it's something to look forward to every day, it was a real treat. We always purchased our weekly celebrity gossip magazines. They were our favourite! We were never short of sweet treats like chocolate, fizzy pop or crisps etc. I think after that I kind of got bored of chocolate because it given me a buzz, but the novelty of it soon worn off.

Some days we attended school which isn't like a proper school, It was just a small area of the unit where we would go to. Obviously, we still had to carry on with our education as normal because it was important to stay busy. Of course, it's not going to be full on as the usual school routines. These sessions lasted about the whole afternoon on most days.

I didn't like attending the little school area although I could see where they were coming from. They were obviously trying to keep us busy instead of moping around all day which if we would attend, it would break up the day a little bit more and keep us amused.

In the evenings, us patients had the chance to go out for a drive around with a couple of the staff. It was something that we would look forward to most evenings. This also included mini trips to the supermarket to buy little bits that we needed like everyday essentials. It was great fun because all of us could choose a film to buy for our unit which we could watch on the weekends. I am a huge fan of movies myself. I enjoy most genres such as, horrors, comedy, action or even children's movies. I am a big kid at heart. I think you're never too old to watch a good children's movie. My all-time movie which brings back my childhood memories has to be Labrynth. The film with the gremlins who stole the baby and the mother must hunt for her baby through a maze with all these fictional creatures, It's brilliant!

Keeping a small diary with me helped also helped. I would write my thoughts and feeling inside a notebook on a daily basis. To get everything off my chest. I also even wrote what I've been up to as well because it kept my mind going through the days. I remember decorating my new notebook I had bought from the shops. My favourite television programme at the time was The Only Way Is Essex. I absolutely loved it! So, I covered my book with stickers of it. My book decorated in TOWIE stickers kept me happy.

Missing home became more often and at times, I felt emotional. I was 2 months into my recovery when I started to feel lonely. My only thought was to keep my mind busy and persuade myself to think of happy memories. It wasn't long until my mum comes up to visit me to take me to London for the day as it was close to where I'm too and it would make a good break away from the usual, same surrounding I've spent a long time in. I felt nervous leading up to the day when my mum came to see me. I don't know why because I should feel myself around my mum. Maybe because it was that I haven't seen her in so long as two months away from home is the longest I've ever gone without being around her.

The day finally arrived after I felt as if I had waited 100 years for this moment. I was super excited to see my mum. Me and my mum are so close, we hardly ever spend time apart. She says that me and her come as one. I'm really surprised she hasn't given up on me after everything that I've put my family through. It just goes to show that family is everything. My mum arrived with her partner after I waited very impatiently in the communal lounge watching the clock tick by. It seemed to go on forever. The wait is finally over I thought to myself. As soon as I saw my mum everything was good. I felt like I was away from her forever. We had loads to chat about! We did a risk assessment and then I was ready to leave for my day out. We caught the train to London which only took 45 minutes. Plenty of time to chat about my stay so far. I said I've met a friend named Bonnie who is lovely. Bonnie is another patient here. We get on like a house on fire. We have very similar interests. We both kept each other entertained with endless amounts of gossiping about the celeb world. That was our main interest.

I really enjoyed London with my mum. It was good although I was out of my comfort zone. Especially as I'm not in the right place at the moment. My mum had noticed that I've lost a lot of weight. This was probably down to stress and cutting down on eating as we only had three meals a day at the unit. It was very rare that we snacked in between. The food there is nice. I was really fussy with food because I don't like a lot of meals. I was very limited and I'd admit that I'm more of a junk food person, I'm not going to lie. I mostly lived on jacket potatoes and sandwiches.

London is such an exciting place but it didn't feel right still. Busy crowds were the worst thing. I hate it when it's busy as I feel really nervous and anxious as if everyone around me was staring at me. I worry what people think may think of me. I'm a very paranoid and conscious person to be fair. Me and my mum took a photo in Trafalgar Square which I look back on now and I feel pretty shocked about as I was so slim when I look back at weight now!

Anyway, my friendship with Bonnie was like a friendship I've never had before. I don't have many friends, I'm not very good at socializing with people. Bonnie and I hit off as soon as we saw each other. We are very similar to each other in ways of our anxiety. Meeting Bonnie is something I will never forget because we knew how to entertain each other and get along with each other although we'd only known each other for two minutes but we felt a connection straight off. I suppose we both helped our recoveries in a way because we met at a bad time in our lives and we've both had to figure out a way of feeling ourselves again which is the most important thing of all.

Time passed and we got to know each other better every day. By now we both bonded over our admittance to the unit because we could tell each other anything because we'd got used to being friends. Bonnie probably made a huge improvement on my recovery and helped a lot which so did I with hers as we helped keep each other's spirits up. You wouldn't think that It would be the best place to make friends but I can tell you now that I made friends that I thought I would never have made. Obviously, a good friendship has their downsides too. I can't tell you that we were always happy and cheerful because I'd be lying if I did. No friendship can have all ups instead of downs. It was rare we did fall out though. It depended on our moods and if we were in our worst moods. We saw each other's ups and downs. It felt like we'd known each other for years and years but that's not true.

We'd fallen out plenty of times by now. It was over stupid, petty situations. Of course we was living with each other 24/7. We knew each other's feelings and we'd push each other's boundaries. It was like living with a sister with that brotherly, sisterly love.

I met another friend named Waleed. He was Arabic and came from an Arabic country although I think he was still living in the UK for some time. Waleed had his own reasons as to why he was admitted which I don't want to break the trust and talk about that. His behaviour was more severe than mine and was his behaviour was more to do with his mental health. I can't exactly remember how our friendship began, however I knew that our issues were kind of similar so that's how we grew close. Waleed I think was a little younger than me. I seem to get on better with younger people as I feel like I don't fit in with older people, in ways of maturity. I can bond a lot more with people who are younger and similar in age. Waleed had his bad days in recovery but that was normal for people like us. He had a lot of anxiety and I think he doesn't know how to control his temper which must be very difficult for him. Waleed and Bonnie obviously knew each other before I had arrived. Me and Waleed was very mischievous. We would cause trouble as that was just about the only thing we could do to keep as amused as we were all very limited in what we could do so to cause some trouble felt good. We would try to escape the unit which we on one occasion. We were sick and tired of not being able to do the things that we normally could do outside of the unit in the real world. We came up with the idea to discreetly and watch one of the staff members tap in the code to unlock the door. We had managed to do it perfectly so we were both wondering if we should run or not. So, as we did, I backed out as I was too afraid although Waleed went. I was a little worried about what might happen in regards to consequences. I was also worried about Waleed. Especially as we're all feeling vulnerable so I decided to tell a staff member for the fear of his safety. I had no choice too. I wanted to be the friend I said I was and look out for them. Waleed then eventually made a return to the unit.

Being in the unit isn't as boring as it sounds. It can be fun too. It's good to have some fun and something to keep you amused while in your recovery to take the edge of seriousness.

I wasn't happy every day as it would be impossible to always be. I had a lot of down moments in there because I was going through a tough time in my life. I was feeling like absolute rubbish which made me want to hurt myself badly because I thought I would never see the light at the other end of the tunnel again. It was at least two months into my recovery where I had suddenly felt my worst as I wanted to see my family as I missed them like crazy, especially my mum, niece, nephew and dogs. Not seeing them for even a week is long enough. I do think I needed the space away but I feel like It was too much time away. Enough was enough now, I wanted to be where I belong which is with my family in an environment I feel most comfortable in. A child at my age should never have to go through something like this. You should be with your family making a recovery because this situation and environment isn't going to be healthy. It's only going to make you a lot worse. You need your family around you for support. There is that saying 'what doesn't kill you only makes you stronger' but that's up to a certain extent. You can only take so much as I did and then that's it you're at your lowest again and it feels impossible to return to your happiest again.

It's tough because you can't let too much anger out of yourself because if you do then it's a big mistake and it'll be too late and even more damage will be done. I strived to have no meltdowns as then I'll be at home a lot sooner. I realised they like to test your boundaries and see how you cope in different situations.

Once I tried to tighten a shower hose around my neck as everything hit me all all at once. It was very hard to hurt yourself in there because everything was so secure and there wasn't a sharp object in sight. Although I did manage to sneak in magazines with staples in to keep the pages together. I took them out and would scratch my arm continuously to take away the emotion in myself leaving my scratches bleed down my arms. I felt a lot better after hurting myself. It's almost like I take it all out on myself because I do still believe now that It was all my fault of putting myself into this situation. Deep down it's nobody's fault as I didn't want this to happen. It just seemed to of got this way because nobody knew what was going on with me until I finally got the diagnosis after all.

I was now diagnosed with Autism and OCD. I still can't believe to this day that I only then got the diagnosis after years and years of not knowing a thing. The services that were involved even accused my mum of being a bad mother for the reason why I was like I am. I felt like they didn't do their job the way they should of. It was horrible to hear how they accused my mum of being an unfit mother. I was disgusted how they could say such a thing. My mum was really hurt, she felt so upset because she then kept questioning her parenting skill although she had always done the best for us children, being me, Charlotte and Lucy, who are my sisters. It never ever crossed my mind that my mum was a bad. It just proves their years of help was a huge waste of time.

My therapy is going well at the moment. The psychiatrists are brilliant. They made sure that our therapy sessions at the unit were as regular as possible and these sessions really helped me unlike a while ago with my local services back in Cornwall who half of the time were never there because my mum had to keep chasing them up and making sure they did their job properly. Mum almost felt as if she was doing the job for them and that's saying something!

By now, I started to question whether I should be here and if it's the most suitable place for me to be in, so I had the rights to appeal to my section 3 under the mental health. I went for it because I had nothing to lose. All I wanted to do was to be with my family so that was the most important reason to why I appealed. Appealing means that you go against your reason for being admitted in the first place. I appealed because I believed this wasn't the place for me. I didn't feel like I was being treated fairly as it I felt I was in a restricted prison. I just wanted my freedom back and to be in the outside world again however when I look back now I'm glad my appeal was unsuccessful because If I didn't stay I wouldn't have got the help I needed however it was a difficult situation to be in even though it was the right decision to make.

I made phone calls home to my family every single night and made phone calls as often as I could. That was the closest I could be to my family. It made me feel happy but very emotional. I'm not usually the type of person to show my love and emotions to my parents, or even anyone in fact, because I feel embarrassed and uncomfortable. Us patients were only allowed to ring our family after 4pm every day and was only allowed a twenty-minute conversation, that's all. Mum would get my dogs to bark out loud so I could hear them down the phone and do it so that I knew they were safe. I missed my dogs a lot. They are like family members to me.

I started to take a liking to the unit's multi-sensory room which was so relaxing. I kind of took advantage of it because at least we had one half-decent bit of luxury although it isn't all like that. We could go into the sensory room most days if we ever needed that bit of time to relax. It was like leaving all of our problems at the door before you enter, the problems that bothered me the most. The atmosphere was lovely and calming. It wasn't a big room, it was only small box room. On one of our activity days, we were allowed an arm massage with real massage oils. The unit's activity coordinator would do the massages. She was a lovely lady. Her name was Evie. Evie was a great listener, I felt that I could tell her anything. We would discuss any issues I had in the unit. There were very many staff who were like this however Evie was the best at talking too. Evie was probably the one who I bonded with the most.

Every day at the unit, it was a struggle however some days were still worse than others. I still felt low and down in the dumps. It was hard to let all your frustration out because it's like you are limited to what you can do and how you release the frustration. It's something I couldn't do here like at home like break something because it would cause you problems such as restraining or being watched. It was like we were all watched 24 hours a day. We had very limited time to have to ourselves without staff checking on you 24/7. I understand that it was there main priority to keep us safe because that's their job but it wasn't like being at home, doing whatever you want as freely as you want to. The healthcare assistants would do their rounds every 20 minutes, depending on what level of at risk you are, they would poke there head through the hatch in the window and ask us if we were ok.

On one occasion I went absolutely ballistic because I felt so frustrated of being shut away from the rest of the world. It actually felt very suffocating although we did get the odd chance to get some fresh air outside but that wasn't all the time and it was a very small restricted area. That was about once in every two days. I'm not going to lie it was tough to be in a small environment even If it sounds like I'm exaggerating but that's being truthful.

Once, it was an evening of feeling stressed because I was bored to the maximum. I suddenly went from being bored to losing my temper because I was fed up and it became too much now. I threatened the staff that I would hurt myself badly if nothing was done about my boredom and anxiety. I felt like they weren't taking any notice of me. I didn't want all the attention. I just wanted to be taken for real instead of looking like the one with issues. I did feel judged sometimes but that was most probably my paranoia which I do get paranoid a lot. I'm always too busy wondering what people think of me rather than be myself. I managed to get hold of a staple from my magazine which I threatened to dig into my throat if they didn't listen to me because I felt I was being misjudged. A few of the night-staff managed to snatch it from my hands and thrown me onto the floor because I put my safety at risk. I was kicking and screaming pleading with them to release me. This went on for a while now. I was on the floor being restrained for around an hour. The staff must of came up with the idea to sedate me because I wouldn't calm down so that was the only solution they could come up with. I was very unaware what they were going to do to help me calm down. They called the unit's on-call doctor in to inject my bottom. This of course made me even more raging. They obviously did warn me that they were going to inject me with some form of liquefied medicine to stop me from tensing and that it would bring my energy down to zero. I was livid. I was petrified to as this has never happened to me before as this came as a shock.

After I was injected with this stuff, my energy came down to its lowest. I became very calm and a little drowsy as It had a huge effect on my energy. I was allowed to get up from the floor and was shown back to my room because I could hardly walk! It was like I was drunk! It felt strange. I was on a totally different planet.

I woke up at mid-night not feeling myself at all. I almost felt strange in some way although I can't describe the feeling. I turned on my light and to find that I suddenly saw strange things. I was in fact, severely hallucinating. I saw snakes in my room on top of my bedside cabinet. It felt so real although I didn't know at the time that I was hallucinating from the injection I was given. I was panicking and was wondering what the hell is happening to me or if this was real or if I was just dreaming.
I walked out into the corridor in the middle of the night walking past another patient's room until I noticed that Waleed's soft tiger teddy was moving slightly, giving me an unusual look. I looked away and

then looked again to have noticed the giant toy, tiger was winking at me. This might come across weird to you but this was what I actually saw, unaware that I was hallucinating and probably just imagining what I was seeing. I went to get a drink from the dining area and stood next to the window sipping my drink. Again, I saw something and I thought my mind was playing tricks with me for the second time. I thought I could see a real tiger strolling around outside on the roof top so I panicked and called for help.

I found a member of staff and told them exactly what I saw. I pointed out to what I thought I had seen but they didn't see anything. They were trying to tell me there was nothing there. Nobody could see it so they told me to go back to my room. I went back to my room and got into the bed until next, I saw even more stranger things happening. This time I strangely saw 3 young dogs in the corner of my room. I shot up and immediately went over to stroke them only to realise that I was touching mid-air when I turned on the light. Every time the light was off I could see these hallucinated surroundings. I couldn't stay in my room any longer I suddenly thought so I moved into the soft room with all the padded cushions which was a cooling down area if you were ever angry. It was so strange and unusual for me. I couldn't quite believe my own eyes. I have never experienced hallucinations quite like this before, it was quite terrifying.

I woke up the next morning feeling confused. I was sure feeling very rough and tired because of the lack of sleep I had and the effect the drugs continued to have on me. By now, it was mid-morning and I had my regular meeting with the psychiatrist. I described what I thought I had seen the night before to which I was told that the hallucinations were quite normal for someone who has been sedated.

Every patient who has been on the ward for so many weeks has the right to appeal against their section, so I went ahead with filling out the forms to request a tribunal where the authorities come together to assess the situation to see if this is the suitable place for me to be kept in. Although I feel like my time in the unit has been helpful to a certain extent, I still felt like I didn't belong here and I shouldn't be in this situation. Yes, I wouldn't have been diagnosed with Autism and OCD if I wasn't here in the first place, but I feel that it wasn't the right place for people with learning disabilities. I should be receiving the help from home in my usual surroundings, the place where I feel safe and secure, not in a mental health unit where they treat mentally ill people. This shouldn't be the case, or at least I should be in a psychiatric unit closer to home instead of being placed six hours away from home for three whole months.

After two weeks of waiting, I finally received a date for my tribunal where I would have to face the panellists and convince them that I am well and that this isn't a suitable place for me to be. I was so nervous in the lead up to the date. I was restless, frustrated and anxious. Clock-watching wasn't going to make time go quicker, if anything, I had to occupy myself and keep my mind busy in order to try not to wind myself up about the prospect of being discharged earlier. I was patient but also excited to see what the verdict would be.

It's Monday now and the day finally arrived. I made sure that I was up way earlier than usual to prepare myself for what's to come. Lunchtime arrived and I had a nervous but exciting feeling that I was going to be discharged. I have very high hopes. It was 1pm on the dot and I have been sitting patiently for the tribunal to begin. Walking into this grand room, it felt daunting. I was nervously shaking and my palms were sweaty, I've had my chance to speak and now my fate lies in these stranger's hands. They knew nothing about me but all I could think was "Have I done enough to convince them I am safe to return back home to Cornwall?".

I was then escorted back to the ward where the other patients wished me luck and they hope I get the verdict I prayed for. Sitting in the communal lounge chatting to the other patients, a girl the same age as I told me that she has been on the ward for almost two years. I was shocked to think that this might happen to me. Am I ever going to get out of here I asked myself? That means I would miss my Christmas, birthday and other family celebrations. She then told me that the last five tribunals she had were all unsuccessful. But, at the back of my mind and deep down in my heart, I still knew that mine was going to be successful.

A few hours passed and that all-important verdict was revealed when I found out that I was unsuccessful this time round. I wasn't upset, I was fuming. I had my heart set on going home and this blew my chances of that. I quickly exploded with frustration and yelled "You can't keep me here any longer!". I ran to the bathroom as quick as I could across the corridor to get away from everyone. I locked the door and for a split second, without thinking, I grabbed the shower hose from the bath and tightened it around my neck. This was it, the moment I had enough. I'm going to commit suicide. I can't take this any longer. The staff retrained me and it took two male staff members to stop me. I was raging with anger and it took me a while to calm down again. When I finally came back around, I realised what's meant to be, will be. I must stick this out just a little longer and I will be back home very soon.

My experience in the unit grew to become a lot worse. I'm half-way through my recovery now and my relationships with the other patients and healthcare assistants became stronger. Having been in there for so long already, I had grown a personal bond with everyone. I didn't want to get too attached to everyone knowing my current situation and the obsessions with people that I've been getting recently.

There's a young male healthcare assistant on the ward who is a major favourite with the patients and is very popular within his place of work. One evening, I had the opportunity to go outside on the hospital's grounds to kick a football around and bond with Simon, the healthcare assistant. As we kicked the ball to each other, he asked me how my time has been on the ward. Using this time to talk openly and honest, I felt a connection as we spoke about why I had been admitted to The Priory. He listened to me with great interest and this was what I enjoyed. I have never had a moment to experience a one-to-one with males because I mainly grew up around females so it was nice to have to confide in another male.

Having spent around an hour on the grounds, we returned to the building. No sooner I returned, I had a phone call. While I chatted to the person at the other end, Simon rushed passed me and gave me a tap on the head and told me it was good chatting to me. This was when my new obsession began. It was the personal one-to-one bonding time and that tap on the head where I felt a connection stemming and he was stuck in my mind and was the topic of my thoughts running through my brain from now onwards. I felt very attracted.

Moving onwards and throughout, Simon was deep in my thoughts and stuck in my mind day and night. This all became sudden and every time I was around him, I was happy but also shy. I started to get jealous when he spent time with the other patients but of course, he had to divide his attention between others too. I needed to realise that it wasn't just me on the ward and I couldn't always have his full attention. I even became jealous when he chatted to his colleagues. I studied so closely that it became clear to me that he was quite close to a female colleague and they were close and friendly towards each other. I would closely observe and stalk his every move on the ward because I had nothing else to do other than sit around and watch TV in the communal lounge.

Things started to change dramatically and by this point even I started to realise that this isn't normal or even doing my recovery any good. In-fact it was making it worse. I was even considered a risk to him and there was talk of Simon moving to a different ward to work in.

I remember an incident that broke out. I was playing on the game console in the communal area where the patients could go to chill out. I had an argument with Simon because I wasn't allowed to take the remote to another room. Instead I refused and carried on to take it elsewhere but as he stood in my way I pushed him. He then grabbed me but as he grabbed I fell over and cracked my head open on the door frame. I was in shock and panicked. There was blood everywhere so I got up and ran to the office to explain what Simon did to me. He was apologising frantically as if he knew he was in the wrong.

I went to the hospital to get stitches on my head; to this day I still have the scar on the back of my head. I blamed Simon for doing it and that it was his entire fault. I was advised to write a complaint but I just couldn't as again, I was too obsessed with this guy and didn't want anything to happen to him so the guilt got in the way and I left it at that.

# Dealing with my sexuality

I have always struggled to know who I am within many aspects of my life, with one being my sexuality. Am I attracted to men or women?

Having grew up mainly around my sisters and without having any friends of my own, as well as me being the youngest, I kind of grew up within a 'girl's world', when I say this, I mean pink, pretty, glitter and sparkles. Always being around my sisters had led me towards being more feminine rather than masculine.

I remember the times when my sisters and I would spend hours playing with Barbie dolls in our bedroom. Even when my sisters had enough of playing with them, I would get the suitcase of Barbie dolls out again and play with them until my heart's content. This was one of my earliest memories.

You would think that a young boy below the age of 12 would be interested in playing with Action Men, video gaming or running around being boisterous. But this wasn't it in my case. I would be the opposite and play with dolls, makeup or host pretend tea parties.

I can remember times when my sister went out to parties with her female friends. While they get ready and glam themselves up for a night out, I would be sitting on the bed watching them do their makeup, hair and choose their outfits for the evening. It was fascinating to watch and I'll always remember thinking 'What if I could be a girl for just one day?'. My answer to that right now is still the same. If I'm being completely honest, I did have thoughts running through my mind that I would transition into a female if I had the chance to.

For days or even weeks, I had thoughts running through my mind about getting a sex change some day when I'm older. I remember it so clear that I would even be researching the internet, 'how to become a female'. I was just a confused teenager having curious thoughts about my sexuality which I didn't know what I was doing at the time because I was too young to know anything about that type of thing. Maybe I just wanted to experience what being the opposite sex would feel like? Even now, I sometimes wonder how it would feel.

I have always looked up to female celebrities more than I have male celebrities. Flicking through my weekly celebrity magazines, I feel a sense of admiration to these women as they're pictured in their bikinis on the beach. I ask myself, what attracts me to them? Do I want to have a female's body or do I just fancy them? That is the question that still sits in my mind now. I'm confused, which makes me question my sexuality.

On the other hand, If I spot an attractive male in my magazines, I would think 'wow, he's good looking'. I personally think that I feel more attracted to men than what I am to women. I have female celebrity crushes but I look at them more as being pretty or beautiful. I don't think I feel physically attracted to them.

I've never experienced being in a relationship with either a female or male but I like to consider myself as bi-sexual because I have never been sexually intimate with anyone before.

I sometimes wonder the thought of getting intimate with someone whether I would enjoy it or not. At this particular moment when I think about getting intimate with somebody, it completely puts me right off the thought straight away. For example, if I was to be confronted by a male or female who wanted to get intimate with me and give me passionate kiss, I would feel uncomfortable. This would be partly to do with my autism. I have a sensitivity towards touching and feeling, therefore, I struggle with getting close to someone. I don't like to be in anyone's personal space or anyone to be in my personal space to a certain extent. It's just an Autistic trait that I struggle with.

Another thing that plays a part in this is personal hygiene. If I was to get intimate with someone and be in their personal space, I would worry and want to be sure that their personal hygiene is up to scratch. They would need to be as clean as possible. It sounds judgemental but that's just what I struggle with, personally. The slightest sign of uncleanliness, e.g. bad breath, sweaty body or aroma can put me off instantly. Why do I feel that way? It's because personal hygiene is important to me and I get extremely unsettled when there is people around me with who don't look after themselves.

# TO BE CONTINUED...

Printed in Great Britain
by Amazon